Air Domain Surveillance and Intelligence Integration Plan

*Supporting Plan to the
National Strategy for Aviation Security*

March 26, 2007

Air Domain Surveillance and Intelligence Integration Plan

<u>Foreword</u>

By issuing National Security Presidential Directive-47/Homeland Security Presidential Directive-16 (NSPD-47/HSPD-16) of June 20, 2006 ("Aviation Security Policy"), President George W. Bush established U.S. policy, guidelines, and implementation actions to continue the enhancement of U.S. homeland security and national security by protecting the United States and U.S. interests from threats in the Air Domain[1]. NSPD-47/HSPD-16 directed the development of the National Strategy for Aviation Security (National Strategy), which established the overarching framework for a comprehensive and integrated national approach to security the Aviation Transportation System, building on current successful initiatives and directing additional security enhancements where necessary, and the following seven supporting plans:

- **The Aviation Transportation System Security Plan** directs a risk-based approach to developing and implementing measures to reduce vulnerabilities within the Aviation Transportation System.
- **The Aviation Operational Threat Response Plan** prescribes comprehensive and coordinated protocols to assure an effective and efficient United States Government response to air threats against the Nation and its interests.
- **The Aviation Transportation System Recovery Plan** defines a suite of strategies to mitigate the operational and economic effects of an attack in the Air Domain, as well as measures that will enable the Aviation Transportation System and other affected critical government and private sector aviation-related elements to recover from such an attack as rapidly as possible.
- **The Air Domain Surveillance and Intelligence Integration Plan** coordinates requirements, priorities, and implementation of national air surveillance resources and the means to share this information with appropriate stakeholders.
- **The International Aviation Threat Reduction Plan** details U.S. international activities to counter illicit acquisition and use by terrorists, other criminals, and other hostile individuals or groups of stand-off weapons systems that pose the most significant threats to lawful civilian and military use of the Air Domain.
- **The Domestic Outreach Plan** ensures stakeholder participation in the implementation of the supporting plans and related aviation security policies and provides guidelines for outreach in the event of a threat to, or an attack on, the United States or another disruptive incident to the Aviation Transportation System.
- **The International Outreach Plan** provides a comprehensive framework to solicit international support for an improved global aviation security network.

While these plans address different aspects of aviation security, they are mutually dependent and complement each other. When combined with critical performance measures, collectively they create the integrated foundation essential for an effective

---

[1] "Air Domain" is defined as the global airspace, including domestic, international, and foreign airspace, as well as all manned and unmanned aircraft operating, and people and cargo present in that airspace, and all aviation-related infrastructure.

strategy and should be regularly assessed to ensure progress in the Nation's aviation security program. These plans do not alter existing constitutional and statutory authorities or responsibilities of the department and agency heads to carry out operational activities and to provide or receive information. Together, the National Strategy and its supporting plans enhance the security of the United States and its interests, including all lawful and legitimate public and private activities in the Air Domain.

Table of Contents

Executive Summary

Air Domain awareness is the effective understanding of threats associated with the Air Domain that could impact the security, safety, or economy of the United States. Achieving such understanding requires close coordination across the United States Government to better integrate intelligence, information, and surveillance data, and analysis related to the Air Domain to facilitate a shared situational awareness across Federal, State, local, and tribal governments and private entities and foreign partners that have aviation security responsibilities. This Air Domain awareness supports a multitude of users across the full spectrum of aviation security and defense activities, including the prevention, response, and recovery activities described in the Aviation Transportation System Security, Aviation Operational Threat Response, and Aviation Transportation System Recovery plans.

Collection, integration, analysis, and dissemination capabilities based on 20th century threats are no longer sufficient. To maximize Air Domain awareness, we must transform, and integrate capabilities that collect, analyze, and disseminate surveillance, intelligence and information to create an operational picture that is tailorable to the needs of users across the United States Government, as well as at State, local, and tribal levels, and with private entities and our foreign partners. This Air Domain Surveillance and Intelligence Integration Plan (Plan) advocates enhanced collection of intelligence, including human and signals intelligence, the integration of all-source information, and the incorporation of computer-assisted anomaly detection to assist human analytic efforts. Further, we must formalize information-sharing relationships, developing a supportive technical infrastructure, and promulgate interagency business rules and processes. Successful execution of this Plan requires a sustained and adaptive national effort coordinated with our aviation security partners at home and overseas.

Ultimately, the backbone of protecting the United States from threats in the Air Domain is an active, layered aviation security and defense. Air Domain awareness, achieved through persistent situational knowledge provided to operational decision-makers, is a critical enabler in achieving this capability.

Purpose

This Plan is an overarching U.S. Government plan that supports and enables the successful execution of the aviation security plans developed pursuant to NSPD-47/HSPD-16. This Plan serves to enhance the U.S. Government's capacity to possess effective knowledge of the threats to the United States and U.S. interests in the Air Domain, including the ability to detect and collect information on aviation threats, integrate and analyze that data in conjunction with associated intelligence information, and disseminate the resulting understanding to deter, prevent, and respond to attacks on the United States or its interests.

The current approach to Air Domain surveillance and intelligence integration focuses on combating 20th century conventional threats by developing creative, but situationally dependent, solutions and connecting otherwise incompatible systems. This approach is insufficient in capability and agility to counter the persistent threat of terrorism, other asymmetric threats, and emerging security challenges. To address this, this Plan directs close coordination across the United States Government to better integrate Air Domain intelligence, information, and surveillance data as necessary to facilitate a shared situational awareness of the Air Domain across Federal, State, local, and tribal governments that have aviation security responsibilities, as well as with our foreign partners. Ultimately, maximizing Air Domain awareness supports a multitude of users across the full spectrum of aviation security and defense activities, whether they are conducting prevention, response, or recovery efforts around the globe.

Scope

This Plan directs the following:

- maximizing Air Domain awareness by improving and developing new capabilities that enable persistent and effective monitoring of all aircraft, cargo, people, and infrastructure in identified areas of interest and at designated times, consistent with the protection of civil liberties and privacy;

- collection and analysis of appropriate data, as well as methods for distributing these to a range of policymakers and operational users, to inform their decision-making about threats emerging either at home or abroad;

- an approach that addresses the threats identified in NSPD-47/HSPD-16, including terrorist-related threats from groups, nation-states, and other criminal and hostile nation-state threats, and the targets and tactics they may employ, including the use of weapons of mass destruction (WMD). The plan does not address ballistic missile or cyber threats, which are covered in other national documents;

- specific department and agency actions to enhance United States Government aviation intelligence and surveillance capabilities in the near-term while forming the foundation and link to ongoing development of future requirements and corresponding solutions for integrated domain awareness and information sharing;

- United States Government departments' and agencies' coordination and sharing of intelligence and other information relating to the Air Domain, but without specifying intelligence and information requirements for individual departments or agencies; and
- the development of shared United States Government Air Domain awareness, built upon the concept of an operational picture tailored to the requirements of the user, which is ultimately compatible with approaches being developed for other domains.

Guiding Principles

- <u>Detection and Prevention</u>. Identifying threats to the Air Domain at their earliest stages of development, using all available intelligence and other information, is paramount for effectively countering them. Such knowledge enables deterrence and prevention activities and supports development of robust plans to deal with these threats if and when they materialize. It also supports prompt and effective warning of policymakers and aviation operators to facilitate operational threat response.

- <u>Unity of Effort</u>. Air Domain awareness requires a coordinated effort within and among aviation security partners, including public and private sector organizations, and international partners. The need for aviation security is a mutual interest requiring the cooperation of industry and government.

- <u>Information Sharing and Integration</u>. Air Domain awareness depends upon unparalleled information sharing. It must have protocols to protect private sector proprietary information and personal privacy. Bilateral or multilateral information sharing agreements, conventions, and treaties enable Air Domain awareness. An information sharing framework that is compatible with and accessible to our domestic and international aviation security partners and secure when required, allows the sharing of relevant, real-time, and accurate information to facilitate decision-making for planned or crisis events, as well as the day-to-day operations for managing the nation's aviation transportation system.

- <u>Safe and Efficient Flow of Commerce</u>. Public safety, aviation security, and the safe and efficient use of the Air Domain for legitimate commercial activities are mutually reinforcing and improved by an effective understanding of the Air Domain. All aviation security partners must act with the recognition that the safe and efficient flow of commerce is enhanced by responsible participation in an accountable system.

Considerations and Assumptions

Considerations
- Threats in the Air Domain are continually evolving and require constant monitoring and adjustments in methods for collecting, analyzing, and disseminating surveillance data, intelligence, and other information.

- Aviation security partners will share information in accordance with U.S. law, Presidential directives, and other national plans and policies, and applicable international obligations or agreements.

- Aviation security partners will consider the strategic importance of international trade, economic cooperation, and the free flow of commerce and passengers when planning for and conducting Air Domain awareness activities.
- Solutions developed to satisfy requirements of this plan and its implementation should be compatible with ongoing efforts of the interagency Joint Planning and Development Office (JPDO) planning and developing the Next Generation Air Transportation System (NGATS) directed by the Century of Aviation Reauthorization Act and the implementation of the Intelligence Reform and Terrorism Prevention Act of 2004.
- Specific implementation actions executed as a result of this plan will be consistent with U.S. law and applicable policy, regulation, and guidance, particularly with respect to surveillance and intelligence activities in the United States and affecting U.S. persons.
- Efforts undertaken in this plan will be designed to the maximum extent practical to be consistent with surveillance and intelligence sharing efforts already in effect or planned for the maritime and land domains. Over time, the goal is an integrated domain awareness architecture.

Assumptions

- Threats may appear at any time with little or no warning. They may take place in single or multiple geographic areas; within U.S., international, or foreign airspace or territory; be conducted in singular attacks or in a multiple, simultaneous fashion; and may result in mass casualties. An aviation threat may exhibit either compliant or non-compliant behavior prior to affecting an attack, adding to the unpredictability of the current threat environment.
- Federal, State, local, tribal, private sector, and international partners will participate and take a collaborative approach, in coordination with the Program Manager for the Information Sharing Environment (PM-ISE), to establish unprecedented information exchange and pooling of resources.
- Existing systems and capabilities will be built-upon and integrated. Systems in development will enhance and contribute to the transformation of these capabilities to reflect changes in technology, policy, and the threat environment.
- The need for security will be harmonized with the imperative to preserve fundamental liberties, especially freedom of navigation, and the legitimate use of the Air Domain for commercial and recreational purposes.
- International participation and cooperation are essential to developing a secure aviation environment, both domestically and internationally. Participation by international partners, while voluntary, requires close coordination on issues such as information sharing and protection, security protocols, and privacy concerns. Personal privacy will be protected as information regarding potential terrorist actions is shared.

Overview

Security in the Air Domain requires a comprehensive and robust, layered aviation security and defense in depth that involves efforts by Federal, State, local, and tribal authorities, as well as private sector stakeholders and foreign partners. The critical enabler for layered security is shared maximum awareness of the Air Domain. Such shared awareness and understanding of the Air Domain, the activities occurring there, and the threats or potential threats to the Air Domain enable the United States to prevent, respond to, and mitigate consequences and expedite recovery from attacks. Maximizing awareness of the Air Domain requires scalable, flexible, transformational capabilities, allowing the United States to detect and collect, integrate and analyze, and disseminate aviation threat information and understanding to operational or law enforcement responders at a maximum time and distance from the United States and U.S. interests. A good example of these elements was the collaboration between United Kingdom and U.S. officials to thwart the August 2006 terrorist air bombing plot.

Air Domain awareness supports core national defense and aviation security priorities over the next decade. Air Domain awareness helps to effectively manage today's complex security environment by:

- detecting, deterring, and defeating threats as early and as distant from the United States and U.S. interests as possible, whether they emanate from abroad or at home;
- supporting sound and timely decisions about, and responses to, the full range of aviation threats;
- enabling shared situational awareness of the Air Domain that integrates intelligence, surveillance, including sensor inputs, reconnaissance, navigation systems, flight data, and other needed information, including information on other critical infrastructure elements such as potential ground targets;
- maximizing shared situational awareness at multiple levels throughout the United States Government, and with domestic and foreign partners and allies;
- facilitating the full application of the law to ensure freedom of navigation and the efficient flow of commerce; and
- supporting the identification, criminal investigation, and prosecution of terrorists, as well as other operational responses to defeat them or efforts to recover from any attack.

Executing Air Domain Awareness

As outlined in the National Strategy for Aviation Security, maximizing Air Domain awareness will require an unprecedented level of cooperation and coordination across Federal departments and agencies as well as across Federal, State, local, tribal boundaries and with private sector and foreign partners. It will require Federal departments and agencies to enhance collection, integration, analysis, and dissemination of data, information, and intelligence available from numerous aviation security partners. The following essential elements shall be utilized by the interagency participants when determining appropriate solutions and implementing this plan, in accordance with the guidance provided in the section below, entitled "Implementation Requirements."

Air Domain Intelligence and Information

The United States Government must enhance its intelligence effort to assess the dynamic set of threats that face U.S. interests in the Air Domain. Surveillance helps to provide an indispensable understanding of the aircraft, people, cargo, and infrastructure in the Air Domain, but it must be integrated with intelligence and other information to aid understanding of current and emerging threats. This understanding may provide the decisive element in determining adversary capabilities and intent in the Air Domain to focus policymakers and operators on the portion of that integrated surveillance picture that is most likely to contain threats, indicate the scale, kind, timing, and location of any potential attack, and inform decisions for deterring, preventing, and, if necessary, defeating attacks.

The Intelligence Community (IC),[2] in coordination with public and private partners, must aggressively use its collection capabilities, including human and signals intelligence, and employ innovative analytic methodologies to provide policymakers and operators with insights about the capabilities and intent of terrorist groups, nation-states, and criminal elements that may seek to use the Air Domain to harm our interests. In addition, regular assessments of threats to the Air Domain are critical so that future threats can be countered.

Under the leadership of the Director of National Intelligence (DNI), the Intelligence Community that supports these objectives must remain highly nimble and agile, with an ability to surge and focus its capabilities to meet increases in adversary activity. Integration of intelligence and information from all sources (State, local, tribal, private entities, and foreign partners) is paramount. Capabilities, policies, and structures must adapt as terrorist targets and tactics change. Operators and intelligence collectors and analysts must closely collaborate to cope with actual threats. A disciplined requirements process must continuously engage intelligence users to ensure resources are applied against the highest priority threats. Intelligence capabilities must be able to surge to cope when threats materialize. In addition to facilitating the development of intelligence and information technology, aviation security partners will, consistent with applicable law, share and integrate existing intelligence and information data.

---

[2] The Intelligence Community includes: the Office of the Director of National Intelligence; the Central Intelligence Agency; the National Security Agency; the Defense Intelligence Agency; the National Geospatial-Intelligence Agency; the National Reconnaissance Office; other offices within the Department of Defense involved in the collection of specialized national intelligence through reconnaissance; the intelligence elements of the Army, the Navy, the Air Force, the Marine Corps, the Federal Bureau of Investigation, and the Department of Energy; the Bureau of Intelligence and Research of the Department of State; the Office of Intelligence and Analysis of the Department of Treasury; the Office of Intelligence of the Coast Guard in the Department of Homeland Security; the intelligence elements of the Drug Enforcement Administration; and such other elements of any other department or agency as may be designated by the President, or designated jointly by the Director of National Intelligence and the head of the department or agency concerned, as an element of the Intelligence Community.

The following specific actions support Air Domain intelligence and information objectives, and as outlined in the roles and responsibilities section below, will be coordinated and carried out by departments and agencies across the U.S. Government that possess the appropriate legal authorities and programmatic expertise:

- pursue means for private partners to proactively share passenger, crew, aircraft, and air cargo data through the development and implementation of expedited Customs clearance for compliant operators, and seek and advance other agreements to enhance information about aircraft ownership;

- continue to refine intelligence collection requirements and analysis towards aviation threats across the Air Domain and conduct periodic reviews to ensure that both the collection and analysis are meeting the needs of aviation stakeholders to enhance Air Domain awareness;

- align, as appropriate, the regulatory and information technology requirements of pre-departure Advanced Passenger Information System (APIS) and Secure Flight for international and domestic passenger pre-screening and for international general aviation passenger and crew vetting;

- use biometric identification technology to assist in identification of employees, including pilots and other flight crew, accessing airport facilities and other critical aviation infrastructure;

- leverage national and international commercial and governmental relationships to obtain manifests for aircraft over-flying the territorial airspace of the United States that are not scheduled to land in the United States, and thus not normally subject to APIS requirements; and

- enter into partnerships with willing nations to identify and monitor transnational aviation threats under existing international obligations and domestic law.

Air Domain Surveillance

To enhance our Air Domain surveillance capability, aviation security partners must regularly assess existing and future sensor requirements and, as needed and where appropriate, Federal departments and agencies must synchronize efforts to develop and integrate new and emerging technologies and capabilities to persistently monitor, detect, identify, and track aircraft in those areas of national interest both within and outside the United States. Leveraging this coordinated effort will enhance the U.S. Government's ability to detect current aviation threats, and also detect potential future cooperative and non-cooperative airborne threats to the United States and U.S interests, including, but not limited to, cruise missiles, low-altitude, low-observable aircraft, and manned and unmanned aircraft systems.

In addition to coordinating the development of surveillance technology, aviation security partners will, consistent with applicable law, share and integrate existing air surveillance data. Integrating available air surveillance data from multiple Federal departments and agencies will enhance the surveillance capabilities of each department while also enabling a comprehensive integrated air surveillance picture of the aircraft in the Air Domain. This integrated air surveillance picture could be shared across the Federal departments and agencies with responsibilities to defend, secure, and operate in the Air Domain. Solutions developed to satisfy requirements for air surveillance should be compatible with ongoing efforts of the interagency JPDO.

The following specific actions support Air Surveillance objectives, which enhance shared situational awareness at multiple levels:

- identify, develop, and deploy new detection and surveillance technologies, including efforts in coordination with foreign partners, and ensure that such development addresses future threats, including those from cruise missiles, low-altitude, low-observable aircraft, and manned and unmanned aircraft systems, as well as stand-off weapons systems such as Man-Portable Air Defense Systems (MANPADS);

- ensure that surveillance coverage must account for aircraft movements on airport surfaces such as runways and taxiways, as well as airport terminals, airside surface areas, and environs, including potential stand-off weapon launch areas;

- bolster surveillance capabilities within U.S. airspace, in the approaches to the United States, and in other areas of national interest through employment of sensor packages, including land-based, airborne, and elevated integrated radar and optical (night, infrared, day) systems;

- improve WMD portable and standoff detection capabilities by synchronizing ongoing United States Government efforts; and

- identify, develop, and deploy new detection and surveillance technologies across North America, utilizing the Security and Prosperity Partnership for North America.

Integrating and Analyzing Surveillance and Intelligence

Integrating surveillance data with intelligence and information improves the understanding and awareness of the Air Domain itself. This awareness enables the United States Government to take appropriate and effective measures to protect, secure, and manage the Air Domain.

Federal departments and agencies will collaborate to develop the technologies, capabilities, and procedures necessary to maximize Air Domain awareness by integrating the air surveillance picture with the data, information, and intelligence related to the Air Domain. This information should include, but is not limited to, aircraft and passenger databases, crew databases, watch lists, cargo databases, terrorist databases, flight profiles, and aircraft characteristics. The Common Terrorism Information Sharing Standards (CTISS) will be leveraged to support Air Domain information sharing. Such efforts will support all-source analysis of specific threats in various dimensions of the Air Domain and enable actions to prevent and respond to potential or actual threats as they emerge.

Federal departments and agencies will also work collaboratively to leverage existing technologies and as necessary, to develop the technologies, capabilities, and procedures necessary to integrate the available intelligence and information with the integrated air surveillance picture to identify and characterize aircraft, determine intent, speed appropriate decision and response times, and enable effective decision making. Solutions developed to satisfy requirements for air surveillance should be compatible with ongoing efforts of the interagency JPDO.

The following specific actions support integration objectives and enhance transparency in the Air Domain:

- Integrate and network existing surveillance systems to enhance shared situational awareness, and ensure that future acquisitions are integrated and networked with appropriate sensor technologies and considers the desirability of combining all domain source intelligence and information;

- eliminate regulatory barriers to information sharing and interoperability through the establishment of operating protocols or Memoranda of Understanding/Agreement necessary for joint, interagency, and industry relationships;

- in accordance with Executive Order 13388 ("Further Strengthening Sharing of Terrorism Information To Protect Americans") and the Intelligence Reform and Terrorism Prevention Act of 2004, determine legal authorities, interagency agreements, and policies necessary to allow the processing, fusion, and sharing of national intelligence, domestic law-enforcement information, and commercial aviation security data with appropriate safeguards, with appropriate surveillance operations centers for ready fusion with surveillance data;

- develop common information technology architecture to support the access and sharing of information across classification boundaries and in a manner that is compatible with such efforts as DoD's Global Information Grid; and

- determine whether sufficient efficiencies and effectiveness are attained by collocating additional intelligence capabilities at the various aviation operations centers, and compare the costs and benefits of this analysis with those associated with maintaining existing facilities and improving connectivity between and among operational and intelligence centers.

The following specific actions support analysis objectives and can help to identify and prevent terrorist attacks and criminal acts in the Air Domain:

- automate processes and collaborative analysis tools for collecting, fusing, and correlating structured and unstructured data to create correlated tracks of aircraft and determine anomalies to assist human analysis efforts;

- analyze information pertaining to aircraft, cargo, and people to ascertain further screening requirements and other protective measures, including for detection of anomalies that may indicate an emerging or imminent threat;

- establish direct data transfers and electronic access to databases, intelligence files, or other repositories for inclusion in the analysis process; and

- develop computer-based algorithms to correlate threat information and merge expanded sensor data and generate automated alerts.

Sharing Air domain Awareness

To be most effective, awareness of the Air Domain must be shared and accessible to aviation security partners at the Federal, State, local, and tribal levels of governments and to the private and public sectors, along with foreign partners. Air Domain awareness requires an information sharing framework that is globally compatible, accessible, and secure. This information sharing framework will provide stakeholders access to net-centric or network enabled, near-real-time, secure, actionable information related to the Air Domain. Solutions developed to satisfy requirements for air surveillance should be compatible with ongoing efforts of the interagency JPDO.

The following specific actions support information dissemination objectives:

- develop an open architecture for data sharing, with standards for web-based information storage and access;
- develop interoperable communication standards among Federal, State, and local partners to enable information sharing, which must be consistent with those developed through other ongoing efforts, including those of the NGATS/JPDO;
- develop information assurance capabilities that allow the sharing of information at all levels of classification among appropriate entities; and
- develop interoperability and information assurance capabilities to enable the transfer of data between sensors, platforms, and people (including assets at the lowest level) to exploit and defeat enemy vulnerabilities.

Department and Agency Roles and Responsibilities

Department of Homeland Security (DHS)
The Secretary of Homeland Security is responsible for closely coordinating U.S. department and agency activities under the national aviation security program. For the purposes of this plan, this responsibility will primarily be accomplished by ascertaining threats, disseminating warning to transportation security sectors and other aviation stakeholders as appropriate, identifying vulnerabilities in the Air Transportation System, and by supporting development of necessary agency and interagency solutions to mitigate the consequences if attacked. DHS is also responsible for establishing civil liberties and privacy safeguards regarding information collected for security purposes. Several DHS components, including the Customs and Border Protection (CBP), Immigration and Customs Enforcement (ICE), Transportation Security Administration (TSA), U.S. Coast Guard (USCG), and U.S. Secret Service (USSS), gather, analyze, integrate, and disseminate intelligence, information, and data to aviation security partners to support law enforcement, operational response, and general security operations in the Air Domain.

Air Domain Intelligence and Information

- The DHS Chief Intelligence Officer (CINT), on behalf of the Secretary of Homeland Security, integrates and manages the Department's intelligence programs. The CINT is responsible for optimizing the intelligence functions of DHS; establishing intelligence priorities, policies, processes, standards, guidelines and procedures, including to support this Plan; and ensuring integrated intelligence support. The CINT conducts periodic departmental program reviews and recommend improvements and/or corrective actions as appropriate. CINT advises and assists the Secretary of Homeland Security and other senior officials in carrying out DHS responsibilities for intelligence activities related to Air Domain surveillance and intelligence integration.

- During National Special Security Events (NSSEs), the USSS is responsible for coordinating the sharing of intelligence, information, data, and awareness with appropriate aviation stakeholders through the NSSE Intelligence Fusion Center. In these instances, the USSS, along with the Federal Bureau of Investigation (FBI), will oversee the coordination and timely dissemination of relevant intelligence information to all departments and agencies with responsibilities in the Air Domain.

- The Domestic Nuclear Detection Office, in coordination with other Federal departments and agencies, detects and reports attempts to improperly possess, acquire, develop, or transport nuclear or radiological materials or weapons in the Air Domain.

- The DHS Science & Technology Directorate, in cooperation with TSA and the JPDO, conducts, sponsors, and enables research, development, test, and evaluation of airport-based and aircraft-borne sensors for detection and identification of WMD and other threats to the Air Domain.

- ICE Intelligence operates simultaneously in multiple environments, including the Air Domain where its main sensitivity rests with the general aviation sector. The ICE Tactical Intelligence Center, and the Albuquerque Special Operations Center, can report relevant information at either the classified or unclassified level.

- TSA receives, assesses, and distributes intelligence information related to transportation security; assess threats to transportation; develops policies, strategies, and plans for dealing with threats to transportation security, including aviation security and airspace security. Additionally, TSA serves as the primary liaison for transportation security to the intelligence and law enforcement communities.

Air Surveillance
- CBP is responsible for detecting and identifying potential air threats to the United States, including aircraft involved in the aerial transit of contraband into the United States. The core of CBP's Air Domain awareness architecture consists of the Air and Marine Operations Center and its specially equipped airborne platforms, which fuse a variety of sensor systems and databases to produce a single, integrated air picture.

Integrating and Analyzing Surveillance and Intelligence
- DHS is responsible for integrating intelligence information and data that will be capable of tailoring database information and search logic with current radar and

other surveillance data. This capability will contribute to the mission of the National Counterterrorism Center for terrorism-related activities (see below).

- CBP's Air and Marine Operations Surveillance System (AMOSS) integrates multiple sensor technologies, intelligence and law enforcement databases, open source information, and extensive communications to cue and coordinate air security law enforcement operations. CBP currently provides a tailored AMOSS workstation to various other Federal Agencies that have a demonstrated need.

- ICE supports the Joint Terrorism Task Forces with customs and immigration expertise. It reviews derogatory intelligence at CBP's National Targeting Center, monitors terrorist watch-listed subjects, and coordinates with the National Counterterrorism Center (NCTC), the Terrorist Screening Center and other agencies.

- In conducting its responsibility for the protection of the President, Vice President, their families, heads of state, other designated individuals, locations, and events, the USSS integrates additional air surveillance capabilities as necessary.

- TSA is the executive agent for, and primary staffing element of, the interagency National Capital Region Coordination Center.

Information Dissemination

- ICE's National Security Integration Center (NSIC) develops and coordinates programs with other law enforcement and Intelligence Community agencies, including utilization of ICE databases and dissemination of threat reporting to ICE field components for action. NSIC includes full-time representatives from TSA's Federal Air Marshal Service (FAMS) and the U.S. Citizenship and Immigration Services.

Department of Justice (DOJ)

The Attorney General is responsible for the investigation and prosecution of terrorist acts or terrorist threats by individuals or groups inside the United States, or directed at U.S. citizens or institutions abroad, where such acts are within the Federal criminal jurisdiction of the United States. The DOJ/FBI National Security Branch (NSB) is responsible under Executive Order and Presidential Directive for counterterrorism investigations and intelligence operations within the United States.

Air Domain Intelligence and Information

- DOJ agencies collect, analyze, integrate, and disseminate intelligence, as well as conduct liaison with other law enforcement agencies.

- DOJ/FBI, acting through the National Joint Terrorism Task Force (NJTTF), facilitates communications, coordination, and cooperation among Federal, State, local, and tribal entities representing the intelligence, law enforcement, defense, diplomatic, public safety, and homeland security communities. The NJTTF interacts with the local Joint Terrorism Task Forces (JTTFs) and provides a point of fusion for terrorism intelligence and support for the State and local JTTFs throughout the United States.

- FBI/Counterterrorism Watch (CT Watch) is an operational component of the FBI Counterterrorism Division at the National Counterterrorism Center (NCTC). It informs and coordinates FBI, Joint Terrorism Task Force (JTTF), and local law enforcement response to terrorist incidents.

- DOJ/FBI/Drug Enforcement Administration (DEA) entities such as the Civil Aviation Security Program, El Paso Intelligence Center, and the Airport Liaison Agents (ALAs) interact and conduct liaison with Federal, State, and local aviation related law enforcement agencies and stakeholders.

Integrating and Analyzing Surveillance and Intelligence

- The Justice Intelligence Coordinating Council (JICC) is responsible for coordinating DOJ's intelligence activities with other law enforcement agencies' intelligence organizations.

- FBI analytical products include Intelligence Information Reports (IIR) and Intelligence Bulletins. The IIR is the standard vehicle through which FBI raw intelligence information is shared with national policy makers and the intelligence and law enforcement communities in support of national intelligence priorities and the needs of law enforcement consumers. The Intelligence Bulletin is a finished intelligence product used to disseminate information of interest, such as significant developments and trends, to the intelligence and law enforcement communities in an article format. FBI frequently issues joint FBI–DHS intelligence bulletins.

Information Dissemination

- DOJ shares information through the FBI Criminal Justice Information Services Division (CJIS), Law Enforcement Online (LEO) network, National Crime Information Center (NCIC) Terrorist Watch List, the planned National Data Exchange N-Dex, and Regional Data Exchange R-Dex as part of the DOJ Law Enforcement Information Sharing Program (LEISP). It also coordinates with international efforts such as INTERPOL to meet obligations under international agreements. These programs aim to ensure Federal, State, local, and tribal law enforcement agencies charged with protecting the public have the information they need to take action.

Department of Transportation (DOT)

The Secretary of Transportation has broad responsibility for the promoting and maintaining the safety and efficiency of the entire U.S. transportation system. The Department's Federal Aviation Administration (FAA) has specific authorities over and responsibilities for the regulatory oversight and operation of the National Airspace System (NAS) as the country's civil aviation authority and air navigation services provider. DOT/FAA also has national defense and homeland security authorities and responsibilities, under which it works in partnership with DHS, DoD, and other aviation security stakeholders.

Air Domain Intelligence and Information

- FAA collects, analyzes, integrates, and disseminates information and data during the normal course of managing the National Airspace System.
- Because FAA controllers are in direct communications with many of the pilots operating in the system, FAA often is the first government agency to be made aware of a possible security incident.
- FAA also maintains a number of aviation-specific databases that contain both real-time and statistical information.

Air Surveillance

- DOT, acting through FAA, maintains the air traffic control system and is responsible for detecting, identifying, tracking, and monitoring aircraft and air vehicle operations in the National Airspace System as it pertains to the provision of air traffic control services.
- DOT, acting through FAA, manages and operates the majority of primary and secondary radar systems that provide coverage in the National Airspace System, including international airspace delegated to the United States for the purposes of air navigation services. While operated primarily for air traffic control purposes, the FAA, in cooperation with DoD, DHS, and other aviation security partners, also utilizes these surveillance systems, as well as linked flight data automation, to support national defense, homeland security, and other law enforcement missions.
- FAA controllers monitor the airspace and aircraft, primarily for safety concerns, but also for security concerns.
- FAA, in cooperation with the JPDO, provides research and development policy for, and description of, future surveillance technologies.

Integrating and Analyzing Surveillance and Intelligence

- FAA correlates automated flight data and aircraft information with aircraft targets for air traffic control and security purposes.
- FAA integrates sanitized intelligence it receives with other surveillance information and disseminates the results at the lowest appropriate classification level to appropriate officials in the field to enhance their situational awareness. FAA air traffic control personnel known as Air Traffic Security Coordinators also monitor the National Airspace System in real-time to assess possible breaches of security.

Information Dissemination

- FAA primarily shares its situational awareness by means of the Domestic Events Network and existing communication lines with current air defense/air security partners. FAA also shares tactical data/radar information with CBP, DoD, and other aviation stakeholders.

- FAA makes this intelligence and information available to most major law enforcement, intelligence, air defense, and homeland security agencies through the Domestic Events Network, and through liaisons at various facilities around the country.

- DOT is the lead agency for the JPDO, and will coordinate NGATS development with DHS, DoD, FAA, National Aeronautics and Space Administration (NASA), Department of Commerce, and the Office of Science and Technology Policy (OSTP). DOT and FAA shall assure that this plan supports the Concept of Operations for NGATS.

Department of Defense (DOD)

The Secretary of Defense is responsible for deterring, detecting, defending against, and defeating aviation threats to the United States and its global interests.

Air Domain Intelligence and Information

- DOD collects, analyzes, integrates, and disseminates defense intelligence, information, and data to support the air defense of the United States and its interests and the sovereignty of its territory. DOD develops, in cooperation with other Federal departments and agencies, sustained, focused intelligence analysis of aviation assets involved in terrorism, weapons proliferation, or WMD trafficking. The Air Force is the lead military service for the national civil air intelligence mission.

- Through the Office of Under Secretary of Defense for Intelligence, DOD develops, coordinates, and oversees the implementation of DOD policy, strategy, programs, and guidance on manned and unmanned spaceborne, airborne, surface, and subsurface activities and other matters pertaining to the Military Intelligence Program.

- DOD coordinates activities that support this plan with the Office of the DNI on matters relating to the National Intelligence Program.

Air Surveillance

- DOD detects, tracks, and conducts surveillance of both cooperative and non-cooperative aircraft necessary for air sovereignty and air defense of the United States and its interests. As part of the United States Government's efforts to integrate surveillance information, DOD makes these capabilities and the data from these capabilities available to other departments as appropriate and as classification permits.

- DOD detects and monitors aircraft conducting the aerial transit of illegal drugs into the United States, required by section 124 of title 10, United States Code.

- DOD develops a networked system of compatible and interactive equipment to provide persistent surveillance, tracking, visualization, and near-real-time reporting of specified suspect aircraft and in areas of national interest.

Integrating and Analyzing Surveillance and Intelligence

- DOD develops capabilities to integrate air surveillance data with all-source intelligence, information, and data necessary for the air defense of the United States and U.S. interests. Where appropriate, DOD works collaboratively with other Federal departments and agencies to develop these capabilities and support U.S. Government Air Domain Awareness.

Information Dissemination

- DOD makes its surveillance and intelligence products available to a wide range of aviation security partners.

Department of State (DOS)

The Secretary of State has several responsibilities that support this plan:

Air Domain Intelligence and Information

- Through its Intelligence and Research Bureau (INR), DOS monitors intelligence reporting on developments and issues affecting the security situation in the Air Domain and keeps the leadership of relevant policy-implementing bureaus and offices in the Department apprised of such developments. INR also provides occasional assessments, as requested or as circumstances warrant, regarding selected developments affecting aviation security.

Integrating and Analyzing Surveillance and Intelligence

- DOS evaluates and grants flight clearance into the United States and its territories for foreign state aircraft, including military aircraft and those aircraft chartered to transport a cabinet minister or other senior foreign government official or other official delegation intending to land in or fly over the United States and its possessions.

- DOS conducts diplomatic relations with foreign governments, including the preparation, coordination, and presentation of demarches conveying U.S. concerns and requests for action regarding the movement or transit of suspect aircraft, cargoes, and persons of interest in the Air Domain.

Information Dissemination

- DOS leads international outreach and coordination with foreign governments for enhanced cooperation in the Air Domain, including on data transfer, and other international advance passenger screening.

- DOS organizes, manages, facilitates, and conducts bilateral, multilateral and international negotiations with foreign governments as well as regional, multilateral, and international organizations to achieve formal agreements on measures, means, and mechanisms for joint or collective actions to enhance the security of the Air Domain.

Office of the Director of National Intelligence (ODNI)

The DNI is the head of the Intelligence Community, principal intelligence advisor to the President, and director of the National Intelligence Program. The DNI oversees the Intelligence Community's efforts to identify and analyze threats to the Air Domain, complement surveillance to detect actual threats if and when they materialize, and conduct other unique missions that promote aviation security. ODNI coordinates with Federal, State, tribal, local, and international partners to promote a seamless intelligence enterprise architecture. ODNI has several responsibilities under this plan:

Air Domain Intelligence and Information

- ODNI oversees the conduct of regular detailed reviews of department and agency intelligence analyses, required coverage areas and levels, and system limitations to inform policy, program, and funding recommendations. ODNI oversees all-source analyses to provide users with the necessary insight to take appropriate preventive, defensive, or operational measures.

- ODNI oversees collection and other intelligence operations of the IC components, including those that gather imagery, geospatial data, signals, human, and open source intelligence related to the Air Domain, including on people or groups with hostile intentions, the movement of dangerous cargo, and the state of worldwide aviation infrastructure. Several agencies are specifically involved in foreign intelligence activities, including the National Security Agency, the National Geospatial-Intelligence Agency, the Defense Intelligence Agency, the Central Intelligence Agency, the FBI, and the intelligence elements of the military services.

- ODNI oversees relationships with foreign intelligence services, which may provide intelligence relevant to threats in the Air Domain.

- ODNI supports recovery from an attack by overseeing efforts of the IC components that contribute to the identification of perpetrators, lessons learned to inform decisions about short- and long-term aviation security measures, and the sharing of analyses with users responsible for plans and operational response.

Integrating and Analyzing Surveillance and Intelligence

- The Director, NCTC, is the DNI mission manager for counterterrorism. NCTC serves as the primary organization in the U.S. government for analyzing and integrating all intelligence possessed or acquired by the U.S. government pertaining to terrorism and counterterrorism, excepting intelligence pertaining exclusively to domestic terrorists and domestic counterterrorism.

- Through DNI directive, the National Geospatial-Intelligence Agency is responsible for providing timely, relevant and accurate information on the worldwide aviation infrastructure, as defined in this plan.

- Through the NCTC, the National Intelligence Council, and other components of the IC, the ODNI oversees all-source analysis about threats in the Air Domain.

- NCTC coordinates formulation and implementation of its analytic efforts within the context of the National Implementation Plan for counterterrorism.

- The ODNI oversees Intelligence Community elements to help identify, based on intelligence reporting, the portions of the air surveillance picture that are of national security interest.
- The ODNI oversees efforts by the Intelligence Community to integrate surveillance data generated by the FAA, CBP, DoD, and other Federal elements with its analyses to enable prudent planning and crisis response capabilities.

Information Dissemination
- Through the PM-ISE, the ODNI plans for, oversees the implementation of, and manages the ISE, which will be a trusted partnership among all levels of government in the United States, the private sector, and our foreign partners to share information to detect, prevent, disrupt, preempt, and mitigate the effects of terrorism against the territory, people, and interests of the United States. Air Domain stakeholder Chief Information Officers and IT professionals and/or Providers, including those working Information Assurance and Security, and Physical Security, shall ensure that their IT capabilities are developed according to the protocols established for the ISE. Furthermore, PM ISE shall develop procedures, guidelines, rules and standards to foster the development and proper operation of the ISE. The PM-ISE will also monitor and assess the implementation of the ISE by Federal departments and agencies to ensure technological consistency and policy compliance.
- The ODNI ensures dissemination of analysis of threats to the Air Domain to policymakers, strategic planners, and operators through a variety of products tailored to their responsibilities.
- Through the NCTC, the ODNI ensures that United States Government agencies have access to and receive intelligence pertaining to terrorism needed to execute counterterrorism plans, perform independent, alternative analysis, and accomplish their assigned activities.
- The USCG, in its conduct of maritime activities, may receive information about threats to the Air Domain, which it communicates with DHS and appropriate Federal, State, and local partners.

Implementation Requirements

Any budgetary requirements resulting from the following directed actions will be addressed within the context of agency, departmental, and government-wide budgetary decision-making processes.

Standardization Requirements

The following actions are directed, in the identified timeframe, upon plan approval:

Immediately:
- DHS, in coordination with the DoD and DOT, shall review and propose any necessary changes to existing department authorities, and policies to determine

primary departmental responsibilities and requirements for detecting, monitoring, tracking, and identifying all aircraft to maximize safety and security within U.S. airspace.

Within 90 days:
- DOT, DHS, and DoD will collaboratively establish a common understanding and, to the extent practicable, shared criteria for identifying security related airspace violations and Tracks of Interest among aviation security partners.
- DHS, in coordination with DoD, ODNI, DOT, DOS and DOJ, shall identify existing department- and agency-level Memoranda of Understanding/Agreement or other documentation that supports sharing of intelligence, information, and data related to aviation security, formalize existing informal working relationships as appropriate, and propose additional necessary information sharing relationships and necessary documentation where gaps in relationships or operational procedures exist. This analysis may identify subsequent efforts at lower levels of authority, e.g., at the regional or office level, as appropriate. A classified annex that addresses relationships and practices in the Intelligence Community or with foreign partners may be appropriate.

Within 180 days:
- DOT, in coordination with DHS and other partners, will articulate recommendations for the development and implementation of an automation system, which integrates flight data, real-time surveillance data, and multiple databases, including aviation, law enforcement, and intelligence sources. This system should enable user defined interfaces, including customized filtering and searches.
- DOT, in coordination with DOD and DHS, will conduct a detailed assessment of department and agency air surveillance capabilities, system limitations, and critical coverage areas.
- DHS, in coordination with DOD, will conduct a detailed assessment of risk in the Air Domain, factoring in identified threats, system vulnerabilities and security consequences, and coordinate an interagency plan to manage that risk.
- DHS, in coordination with DOD, DOT, DOJ and ODNI/CIO, shall conduct a joint assessment of current connectivity capability and requirements and develop a plan to enhance connectivity among their air operational centers to physically enable more effective information sharing. This Plan shall identify requirements for the necessary communications, data, and imagery that need to be shared and the appropriate method for sharing it.

Planning Requirements
The following actions are directed, in the identified timeframe, upon approval of this Plan:

Within 180 days:

- DHS, in coordination with DOD, DOJ, and DOT, shall analyze the advantages and disadvantages of consolidating intelligence capabilities at the aviation operations centers.
- ODNI shall review, in the context of the National Intelligence Priorities Framework, the intelligence collection requirements associated with aviation security to ensure that priorities and collection efforts are appropriately allocated. Adjustments to the requirements will be made in accordance with standard operating procedures and processes.
- ODNI, in coordination with DHS, DOD, and DOT, shall propose a framework to further facilitate surveillance and intelligence integration. This framework shall include identification of leadership and authorities, as well as development of appropriate rules and standards, for the collaborative interagency and international intelligence enterprise that is the cornerstone of Air Domain intelligence integration.

Within one year:
- DOT, in coordination with DOD, DHS, JPDO, and other aviation security partners, shall develop a coordinated air surveillance implementation plan, which recommends solutions to address any gaps in aviation security requirements. At a minimum, this plan shall address the following:
  - maintenance and improvement of current air surveillance capabilities;
  - options for enhancement of current air surveillance capabilities for low altitude coverage in areas of national interest;
  - interagency responsibilities to detect, monitor, track, and identify all aircraft, both cooperative and non-cooperative, in or approaching U.S. airspace;
  - recommended solutions, including those associated with cost sharing, to address identified surveillance gaps;
  - development of next generation surveillance and detection capabilities;
  - transition to future surveillance capabilities; and
  - appropriate agencies to implement the plan within a specified timeline.

- DHS, in coordination with DoD and DOT, shall develop a plan to integrate the air surveillance data made available from all Federal departments and agencies and private sector entities, into an integrated air surveillance picture, definable by the end-user. This plan should be informed by and mutually supporting of ongoing efforts, including those of the NGATS/JPDO and PM-ISE. At a minimum, this plan shall address:
  - minimum standards;
  - technical requirements to share information;
  - resourcing and prioritization;
  - security standards;
  - interoperability;

- o future integration of maritime and land domain surveillance, intelligence, and all-source information to create all domain awareness;
- o implementation timelines, and corresponding department and agency roles and responsibilities;
- o integration of surveillance and other useful data, such as geographic information system compatible data, on pertinent ground features and activity outside of the Air Domain;
- o mechanisms to support user defined operational pictures, which draw from shared data sets.

- ODNI shall promulgate policy and guidance for intelligence integration for the Air Domain and ensure compatibility with approaches for other threat domains. This includes setting business process rules, technical standards, and mechanisms for adjudicating interagency conflicts.

Performance Measures

DHS, in coordination with DoD, ODNI, and DOJ and other appropriate departments and agencies, will develop and implement the following within 180 days:

- baseline assessments of surveillance capabilities, and the adequacy and integration of intelligence information;

- aviation surveillance and intelligence evaluation mechanisms that regularly assess the adequacy of the air surveillance and intelligence integration capabilities and information sharing protocols, iincluding an assessment of necessity and feasibility of an all-domain, all-source surveillance and intelligence integration and information sharing capability across the United States Government and with its security partners; and

- a comprehensive observations and lessons-learned methodology that provides ready feedback to appropriate agencies in response to identified current or future gaps in surveillance or intelligence.

Summary

The United States faces a complex, dynamic strategic environment. We are engaged in a global war on terrorism and confronted with traditional nation state threats. These challenges to our security and economic livelihood require a new mindset – one that sees the total threat and takes all necessary actions through an active, layered defense-in-depth.

The effectiveness of the U.S. aviation security efforts relies greatly on measures to deter and prevent adversaries who intend to do us harm from acquiring the access, tools, and wherewithal to carry out an attack. In the event these measures fail, the United States Government will be in the right position with the right capabilities to resolve, or if necessary as a last resort, defeat threats to the United States or U.S. interests in the Air Domain. Air Domain awareness is a critical enabler for the effective execution of these security and defense prevention and response activities, as well as to inform senior government officials in their decision-making associated with recovery from an attack on the United States or other disruptive incident to the Aviation Transportation System.

The Air Domain Surveillance and Intelligence Integration Plan sets forth the path toward maximizing awareness and understanding of the Air Domain and ensuring its effectiveness in meeting national requirements. The implementation of this plan will not be accomplished over a period of months, rather will be continuous and will require the continued investment of our Nation's intellectual, technical, and financial resources, implemented in coordination with our State, local, tribal, private, and foreign partners.